HIDING

by Karen Wallace and Charles Fuge

W

All animals hide.
They change their colour.
They change their shape.
They pretend to be
something else.
These ways of
hiding are called
camouflage.

A horned frog who looks just like a leaf will be safe in the forest.

You can discover the secrets of camouflage. Some of them are hidden in this book!

A speckled coat hides this baby deer in shadowy woodland.

This stone fish rests among stones but his poisonous spine keeps his enemies away.

Animals hide so they can attack without being seen.

WATCH OUT for this tiger!

Do you think this crocodile looks like a log?

4

A polar bear hides her black nose so she is almost invisible against the snow.

A sloth's fur is covered in lichen and moss. She is as green as the tree she lives in.

6

Animals use their colour to hide from their enemies.

A tawny frogmouth closes his eyes and pretends he's a branch.

And this caterpillar looks like a bit of twig.

Some African butterflies
hide by living in clusters.
Some of them taste nasty.

Some of them don't.
But a hungry bird
doesn't like to risk
making a mistake!

You would have to look a long time to find these chameleons. They can change their skin to almost any colour!

These African chameleons keep very still. They eat tiny bugs who don't notice them in the leaves.

Eyes can give the game away!
Hide them and no-one
will eat you!

An angel fish and
a butterfly fish hide their
eyes behind a black stripe.

When a raccoon prowls
at night, he doesn't
want anyone
to see him.

12

Eyes can protect you if you have fierce pretend ones.

KEEP AWAY!

This frog's bottom is watching you!

13

This sponge crab hides by pretending he's a sea sponge.

Don't tell anyone but there's a hermit crab living here.

14

Some animals decorate themselves so nobody knows they are there.

An African bug covers itself in ant bodies so it doesn't look tasty to its enemies.

Many animals pretend they are plants so they can hide and stay safe.

This leaf insect sways like a leaf. Could you tell the difference?

Who wants to eat thorns? These thorn bugs can fool a hungry bird.

An Australian leafy seadragon looks like a piece of seaweed. You'd have to look carefully to see him.

17

Sometimes harmless insects look like harmful ones so their enemies won't eat them.

Each one is pretending to be a wasp, a hornet or an ant with a nasty sting.

This harmless Malaysian keelback flattens his neck and pretends to be a deadly snake like a cobra.

21

Nobody wants to eat you if they think you are dead already!

An opossum pretends to be dead because most of its enemies don't eat dead animals.

A grass snake rolls on its belly and lets its mouth hang open.

If you were a bird would you eat this click beetle?

Birds lay specially coloured eggs so their enemies won't see them.

Can you see this little tern's eggs?

Dogfish egg sacs are called mermaids' purses. They look just like seaweed.

24

This mother cuckoo has stolen a reed warbler's egg and laid her own in its place.

Can you spot the cuckoo's egg? This reed warbler can't.

25

Some baby animals have special colours to keep them safe from their enemies.

A stripey coat helps wild boar piglets blend in with the shadows.

When a young zebra stays close to his mother he is almost impossible to see.

A harp seal pup is white as the snow around him.

27

All animals hide.
Who is hiding here?

More information

Angel fish – the black pretend eye on the fish's back is there to trick enemies and draw attention away from its head (page 12).

Baby deer – as it grows bigger and stronger the coat loses its speckles (page 3).

Chameleon – a chameleon flicks out a long sticky tongue to catch unlucky flies (page 10-11).

Crocodile – a crocodile can wait without moving for a long time. This helps him to trick other animals (page 4-5).

Cuckoo – the cuckoo lays one egg at a time in different birds' nests. The egg is slightly larger but looks like the other eggs (page 25).

Harp seal pup – when a pup is old enough to swim he loses his white coat and turns a mottled grey (page 27).

Hermit crab – this crab lives in many different sorts of shells. As it grows bigger it simply moves "house" (page 14).

Leafy sea-dragon – he is a kind of seahorse. He looks so much like a piece of floating seaweed that small fish hide behind him (page 17).

Opossum – playing dead does not keep it safe from all animals (page 22). Hyenas and vultures like to eat dead things. They are called scavengers.

Raccoon – a raccoon is a nocturnal animal which means it is active at night and rests during the day (page 12).

Vine snake – it kills its prey by injecting a small amount of poison from its fangs at the back of its mouth (page 18-19).

To Miranda

First published in 1998 by Franklin Watts
96 Leonard Street
London EC2A 4XD

Franklin Watts Australia
14 Mars Road
Lane Cove
NSW 2066

This edition 1999

Text © 1998 Karen Wallace
Illustrations © 1998 Charles Fuge
Series editor: Paula Borton
Art director: Robert Walster
Consultant: Dr Jim Flegg, Institute of Horticultural Research
Printed in Singapore
A CIP catalogue record is available from the British Library
ISBN 0 7496 2905 3 (cased)
ISBN 0 7496 3443 X (paperback)